Riffs, Chords & Tricks
you can learn today!

▶▶ Fast *Forward*™

with Rikky Rooksby

Blues
Guitar

EXCLUSIVELY DISTRIBUTED BY

HAL•LEONARD®

Exclusive Distributors:
Hal Leonard
7777 West Bluemound Road,
Milwaukee, WI 53213
Email: info@halleonard.com

Hal Leonard Europe Limited
42 Wigmore Street,
Marylebone, London WIU 2 RY
Email: info@halleonardeurope.com

Hal Leonard Australia Pty. Ltd.
4 Lentara Court, Cheltenham,
Victoria 9132, Australia
Email: info@halleonard.com.au

Order No.AM951160
ISBN 0-7119-7041-6
This book © Copyright 1998 by Hal Leonard

Book design by Michael Bell Design.
Edited and arranged by Rikky Rooksby.
Music processed by Barnes Music Engraving.
Cover photography by George Taylor.
Cover instrument kindly loaned by World Of Music.

Text photographs courtesy of
London Features International.

Printed in the EU

www.halleonard.com

Introduction

Hello, and welcome to ▶▶**Fast*Forward***

Congratulations on purchasing a product that will improve your playing and provide you with hours of pleasure. All the music in this book has been specially created by professional musicians to give you maximum value and enjoyment.

If you already know how to 'drive' your instrument, but you'd like to do a little customising, you've pulled in at the right place. We'll put you on the fast track to playing the kinds of riffs and patterns that today's professionals rely on.

We'll provide you with a vocabulary of riffs that you can apply in a wide variety of musical situations, with a special emphasis on giving you the techniques that will help you in a band situation.

That's why the music examples in this book come with full-band audio tracks so that you get your chance to join in. All players and bands get their sounds and styles by drawing on the same basic building blocks. With ▶▶**Fast*Forward*** you'll quickly learn these, and then be ready to use them to create your own style.

Playing Blues Guitar

It seems everyone likes blues – it's a universal music. Three chords, 12 bars – such a simple musical form capable of being presented in so many ways. Getting to grips with the basics of blues guitar isn't difficult – that's where this book will help you. Maybe you've already learned some scales, yet nothing seems to come together properly. This book will show you how to make the most of what you already know and start playing blues solos.

Although an Eric Clapton, Jeff Healey or Stevie Ray Vaughan in full flight may make it seem as though you've got to be able to play loads of notes, that isn't really the case. Contrary to what you may have feared, you don't need a fierce technique and the ability to reel off 600 notes a minute to play a good blues solo. Good blues guitar playing is expressive. It communicates an emotion through the particular musical language of the blues. The first requirement of a blues guitar solo is that it must make musical sense, not that it should be technically complicated or impressive.

In this book you will find examples of blues guitar solos. Most of them are 12 bars long , but you'll also have the opportunity to solo for longer. Anyone with a couple of scale patterns can widdle away for several minutes piling phrase on top of phrase, but a good solo needs shape. It's good discipline to learn how to say what you have to say in a short timespan. Certainly, in the studio most solos are fairly short – only in the club or concert hall is there the time and opportunity to stretch out.

This book will give you ideas on scales, how to phrase, and a host of other tips to help you to put together effective blues guitar breaks. The music has been composed so that relative beginners and intermediate players will be able to progress throughout. However, it does assume some basic knowledge of musical notation and guitar techniques – if you are new to blues playing, I recommend that you also get a copy of ▶▶**Fast*Forward*** *Classic Blues Guitar Licks.*

Rikky Rooksby

Each example is given in musical score and in guitar tablature. With the latter each number indicates the fret at which the note is played – each line represents a string. If you find it hard to remember which way up they go, think always of pitch: high notes are above low notes, therefore the high-sounding string (1st E) is at the top. Underneath the TAB you will find suggested left-hand fingerings (index = 1, middle – 2, ring = 3, little = 4). Other TAB symbols will be explained as we go along.

Each musical example is played once with the lead guitar, and once without. The first is for you to learn by listening, the second 'play-along' track is for you to practise.

The examples have a one-bar count-in.

 TRACK 1: TUNING NOTES

The Five Note Trick
Exercise 1: The Pentatonic Minor

You only need five notes to play through a 12-bar. Don't believe it? Read on...

Playing good blues solos depends on musical understanding. It's not only what you know, but knowing how to apply it. The first example will surprise you – we're going to start with a very simple idea and then show you what can be done

with it. We're going to take only five notes – E G A C D and play through an entire 12-bar sequence. These five notes form the scale of A pentatonic minor (A C D E G). The pentatonic ('five-note') scale is the most common in blues, and in Part 2 we'll be looking at the scale in more detail. The backing is a 12-bar blues in the key of A major.

TRACKS 2+3

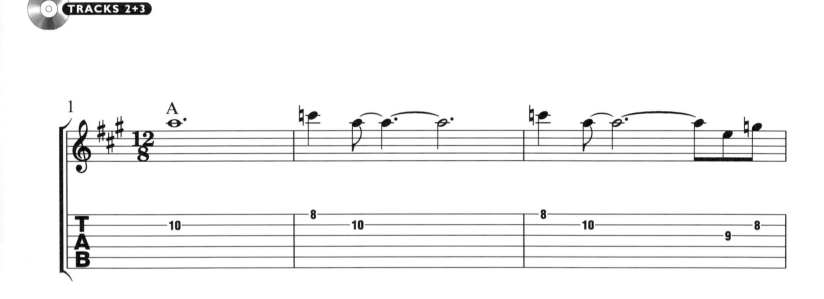

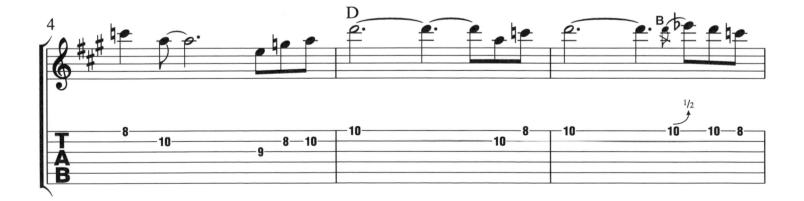

Notice how the first 4 bars use just a few notes and let them ring for a number of beats. At bar 5 the chord changes to D. The D in the lead break sounds effective because it's the 'root' note of the chord over which you're playing. In bar 6 you'll notice a bend – the D note is pushed up a semitone to E♭. This note is known as the flattened '5th' (♭5) and is one of the 'blue notes' which gives the blues scale its distinctive sound.

String-bending

String-bending is vital to blues guitar. When bending strings remember to support the finger which is actually doing the bend by putting the preceding fingers on the same string on the immediate lower frets. If you're bending with your first finger this won't be possible, but if you're using your second or third fingers, put the first and second down too. The little finger is very rarely used for bending.

Exercise 2: The Pentatonic Major

Exercise 1 gave us a typical blues sound. The minor scale clashed with the major chords of the backing and this created the sound which the ear interprets as the blues. Now we are going to bring in a magic formula of blues guitar:

If you move a pentatonic minor scale pattern down three frets it will convert to the major pentatonic on the same root note.

In example 1 you were playing at the 8th fret – if you go down three frets to the 5th fret, you will now have the notes C♯ E F♯ A B. Assembled into the right order – A B C♯ E F♯ – these are the notes of A pentatonic major. Try Exercise 2 and you will hear the difference in mood this creates.

TRACKS 4+5

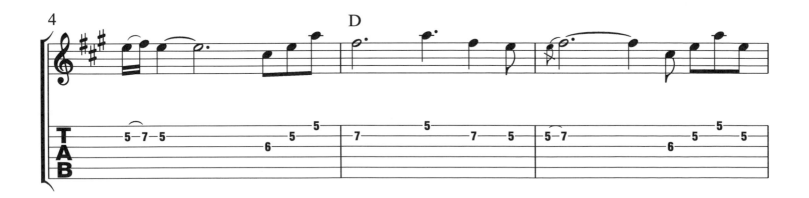

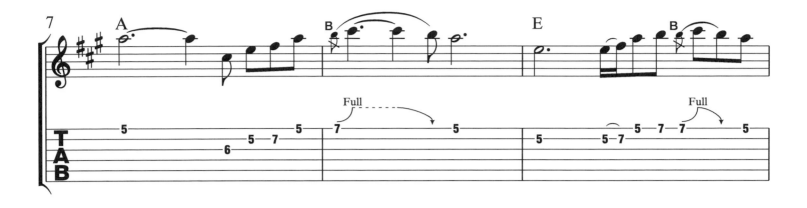

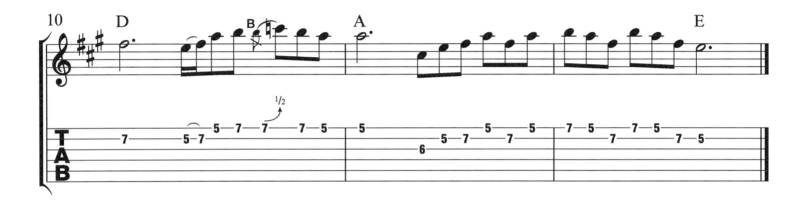

The bend in bar 1 from B to C♯ is a common one in this position – it allows you to use an extra note without having to move anywhere. Bar 8 features a bend with a slow release – make sure you keep your finger pressed to the fretboard while the note is ringing otherwise you may cause it to die.

Notice that bars 1 and 3 are identical – repetition is essential to all forms of music, especially the blues. Never be afraid of repeating a phrase – students learning lead guitar often make the mistake of playing streams of notes, wandering over the fretboard, leaving nothing for the listener to hang onto. To play and then repeat a phrase gives the listener the pleasure of recognising something. Watch out for repeated phrases, they are used throughout this book.

Exercise 3: Mixing Major And Minor

What you're going to do now is to play a
12-bar blues which mixes the two scale positions
you've learnt so far. This is an important blues
technique. Listen for the way that the sad minor
phrases at the 8th fret contrast with the brighter,
happier tone of the major scale phrases at the
5th fret.

TRACKS 6+7

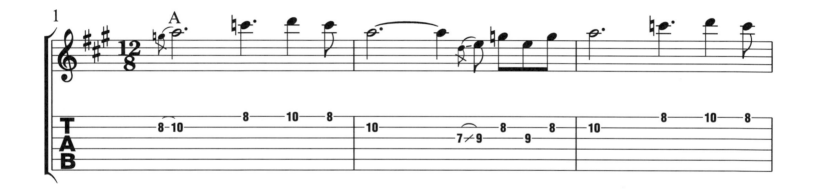

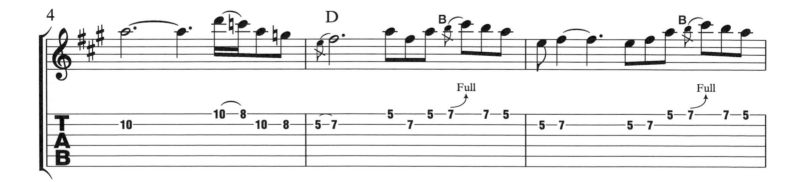

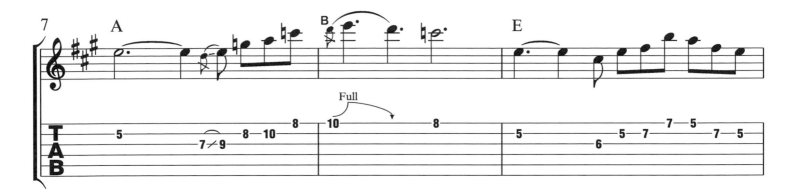

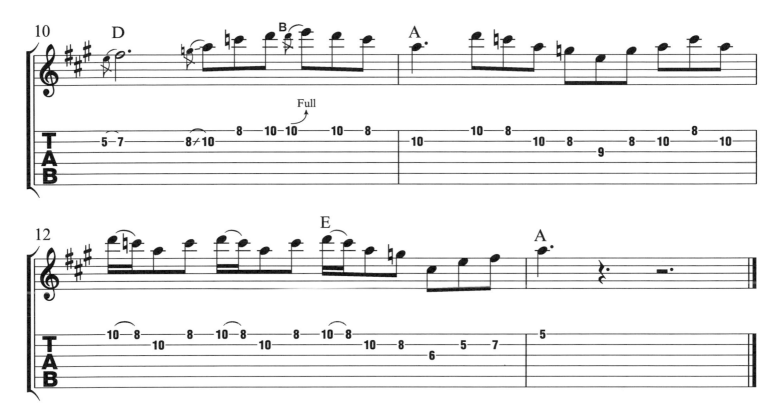

Bars 1-4 use the pentatonic minor. At bar 5 (just in time for the change in the rhythm chords to D), the solo shifts down to the A pentatonic major at the 5th fret. In bars 7 and 10 a slide (marked ⌒) enables you to make a quick shift from one scale to the other. To give the solo a twist in the tail, the last beat of bar 12 features notes from the major pentatonic after a long run of minor notes.

Exercise 4: The Pentatonic Minor Shift

Compared to playing lead solos in other types of music, playing blues solos with these pentatonic scales is easy. That's because the 12-bar chord structure is 'forgiving' when combined with these scales. You can play any of the notes of the pentatonic scale without anything sounding hideously wrong (although it is true that some will sound better than others).

You don't need to worry that there will be an awful clash if you hit the wrong note!

However, it is possible to play and take account of the changing chords. A 12-bar blues usually features three chords: the key chord (chord I), the sub-dominant (chord IV) and the dominant (chord V) in whatever key you're playing in.

A major

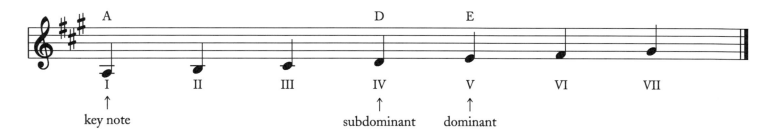

The roman numerals refer to the degree (or note) of the major scale that these chords are built on. All the examples so far have been in the key of A so we need to refer to the scale of A major (given above). Chord I is based on the first note of the scale (the key note), A, and is therefore called A major. Chord 4 is built on the 4th note of the scale, and is therefore D major, and chord V is E major.

In Exercise 4 we are going to be more adventurous and shift position and scale in time with these chord changes.

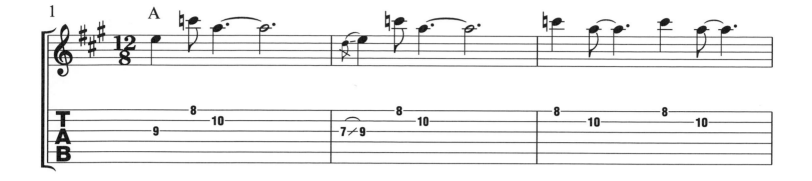

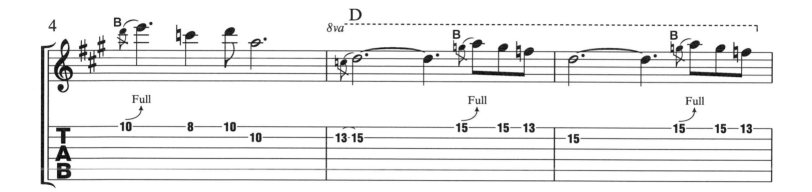

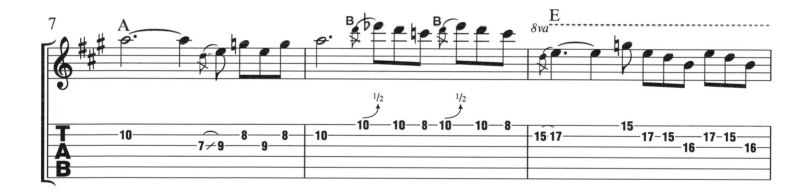

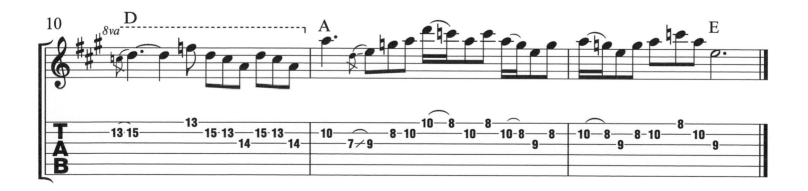

▶▶ ERIC CLAPTON
"Otis Rush, Buddy Guy ...it's not so much technique that I listen for; it's the content really, and the feeling and the tone."

You'll notice immediately that this example has a more varied sound than the examples which only used the A scales. At bar 5, the backing band moves to the chord of D major, and so the scale changes to D pentatonic minor at the 13th fret. The *8va* symbol above the music at this point simply means that the notes sound an octave higher than they are written on the musical stave.

D pentatonic minor is just the A pentatonic minor scale position you've been using at the 8th fret shifted up 5 frets to the 13th fret (8 + 5 = 13).

At bar 7 the solo returns to A pentatonic minor as the chord goes back to A major. When you reach the chord of E major at bar 9, you then need to move up 7 frets to the E pentatonic minor scale at the 15th fret (8 + 7 = 15).

As the chord drops to D major in bar 10, we shift down two frets back to the D pentatonic minor scale at the 13th fret, before finishing where we started, back at the 8th fret.

Note that in most types of music it is inadvisable to play a minor scale in a major key or over major chords. Blues music tolerates this – it is the clash of the minor notes against the major chords which creates the distinctive 'flattened' effect of blues music.

▶▶ **VAN HALEN**
*"I don't go outside of blues scales all that much. I don't do anything that weird.
I don't know what it is I do. It's just rock'n'roll, and most rock'n'roll is based on blues."*

Exercise 5: The Pentatonic Major Shift

In this exercise we are going to use the same
principle of shifting scale positions to match the
chord changes, but apply it instead to the
pentatonic major scales.

TRACKS 10+11

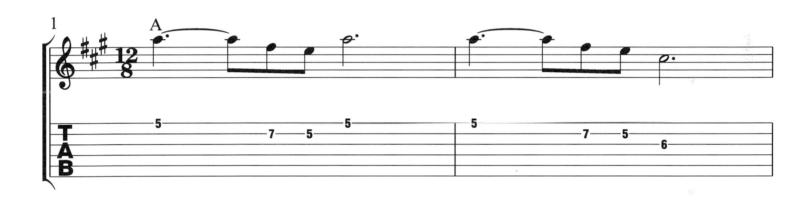

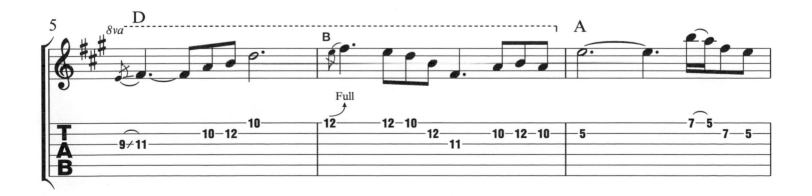

►► JOHN LEE HOOKER

"If you're playing blues, play with your heart and ears. The blues isn't in the book, you've got to feel it. If you don't have the feeling and rhythm, you can forget it."

As with exercise 4, the shifting positions produce a more varied sound than the examples which only used the A scales. The major scales sounding over a major chord backing results in a happier mood, but you won't hear the emphasised blues effect created by the clash of the minor pentatonics against the major backing.

Once again, at bar 5 the backing moves to D major and so the scale moves to D pentatonic major at the 10th fret. This is the A pentatonic major scale position you've been using at the 5th fret shifted up 5 frets (5 + 5 = 10).

At bar 7 the solo returns to A pentatonic major as the chord changes back to A major. With the chord of E major at bar 9 the solo moves to the E pentatonic major scale at the 12th fret.

As the chord drops to D major in bar 10, you shift down two frets to the D pentatonic major scale before finishing with a brief return to the 12th fret E scale.

The pentatonic major is a 'forgiving' scale in a major key. You may use it in any style of music in a major key and it will sound effective. However, you cannot play it in a minor key – the clash of the major notes against the minor chords is simply discordant. If you would like to hear for yourself, try playing these scale positions over the backing for the minor-key piece in Part 3 called *After The End* (Track 35).

Exercise 6: The Major–Minor Overlap

To complete this section we will introduce another concept. All the soloing you have been doing so far has been based on one basic five-note 'box' shape on the top three strings. You've learnt how to move this shape to different positions in order to make it fit the changing chords, whether they are major or minor. But there are many different shapes like this one. In Exercise 2 you learned that shifting a pentatonic minor down three frets converts it into the pentatonic major on the same note.

Here is another important new idea:

If you are playing in a pentatonic minor scale position, the notes of the pentatonic major overlap in that same position, and vice versa. This means you can change scale without changing position, simply by using a different pattern of notes.

Try Exercise 6:

TRACKS 12+13

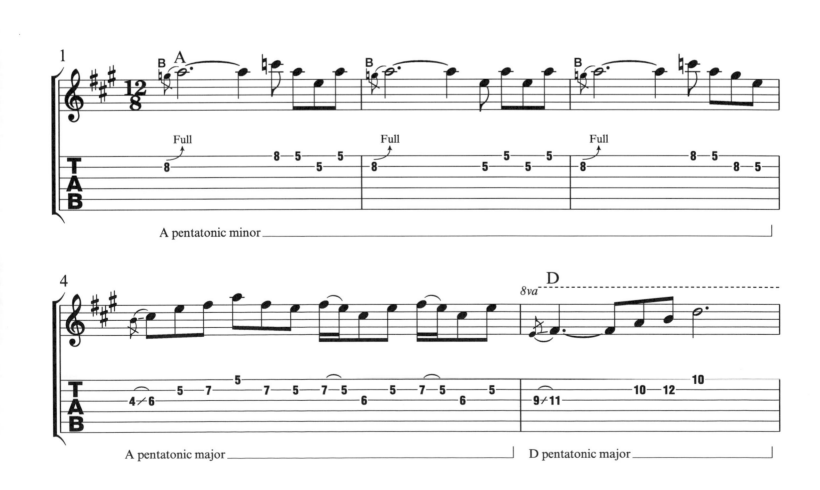

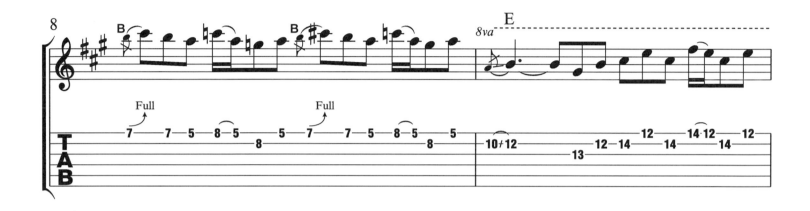

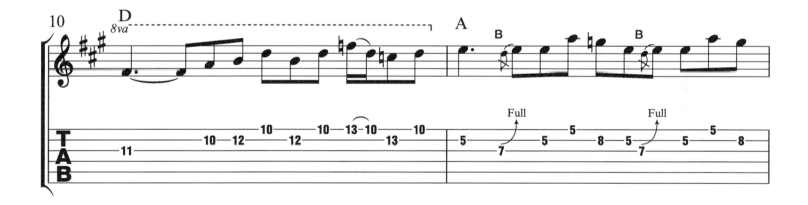

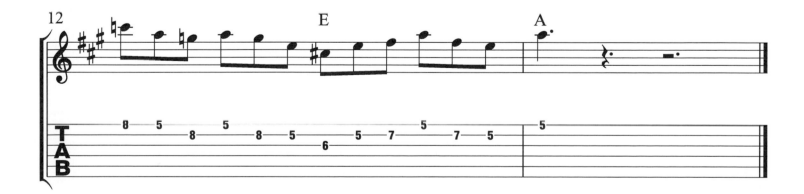

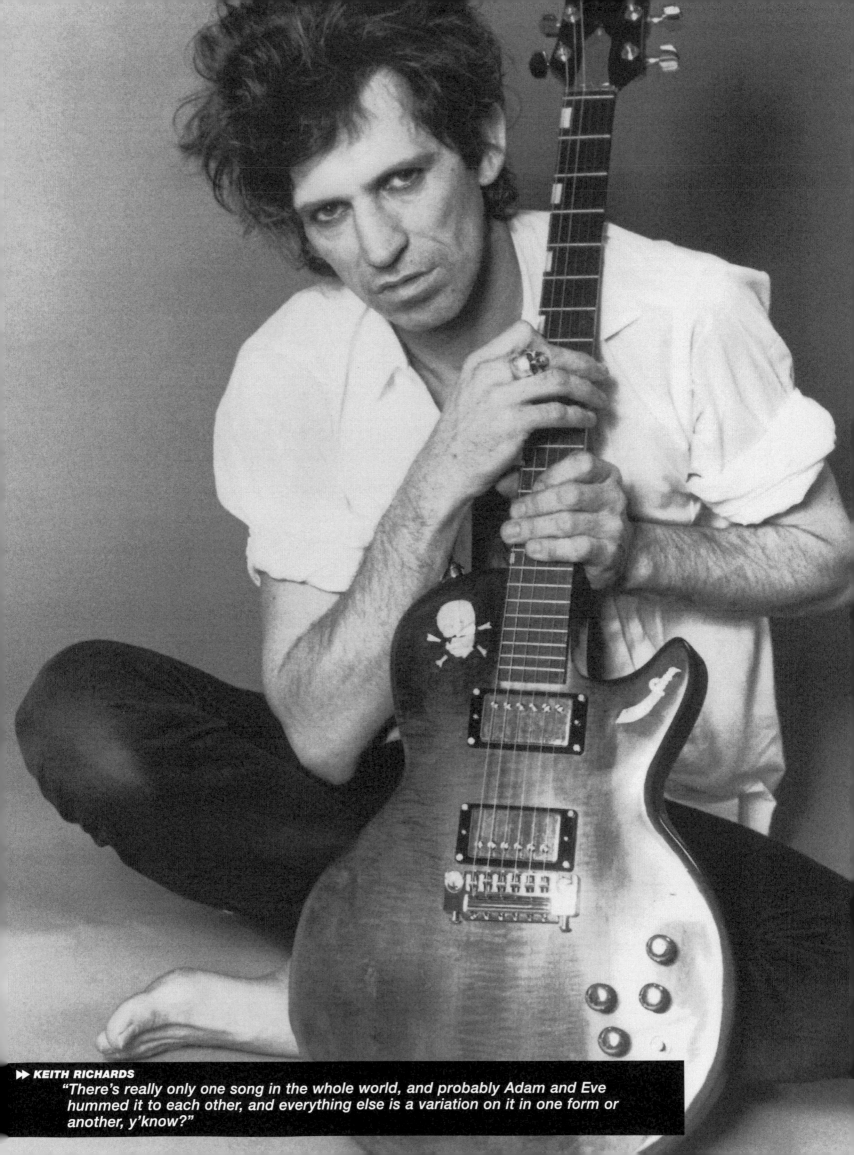

▶ **KEITH RICHARDS**
"There's really only one song in the whole world, and probably Adam and Eve hummed it to each other, and everything else is a variation on it in one form or another, y'know?"

In bars 1-3 you're playing an A pentatonic minor pattern at the 5th, (instead of the 8th fret which you have used before) but in bar 4 this changes to A pentatonic major without moving up or down the neck. In bar 5 the solo moves to D pentatonic major at the 10th fret and then changes to D pentatonic minor in the same position. Notice the last four notes in bar 6 – these represent a switch of scale back to the major. Similarly, in bar 10 D pentatonic major becomes minor for the last 4 notes. In bars 8 and 10-11 major phrases alternate with minor ones, creating a dramatic contrast.

At once simple, and yet capable of so many combinations: this is the fascination of blues guitar.

Scales – The Alphabet Of The Blues

Although there are many types of scales, the majority of blues solos are performed with only a few. Not only that, they are generally played in the same positions and use the same patterns. Since the most common keys for blues music are E major, A major, E minor and A minor, the examples in this book are in these keys. Why should this be? Well, what are the guitar's lowest open strings?

Answer: E and A. These keys enable you to use these low notes and other open strings. The guitar resonates in E more than in any other key. All the solos in this book will be played with the scales described in this section.

Here is the scale of A pentatonic minor with the root note on the 6th string.

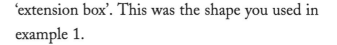

TRACK 14

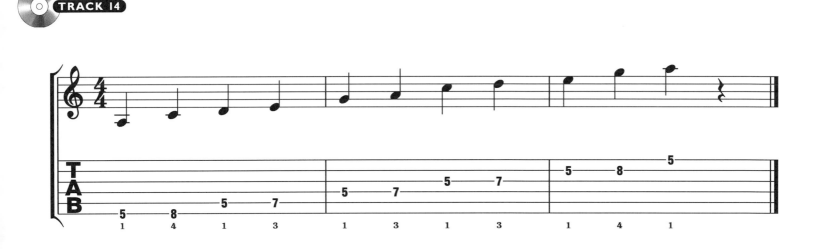

Here is the same scale with a slight change of position that allows you to go a little higher up the neck. I call the last six notes of this the 'extension box'. This was the shape you used in example 1.

TRACK 15

Here is the same scale starting with the root note A on the 5th string. This version of the scale sounds much higher.

 TRACK 16

By inserting one extra note – E♭ (the flattened 5th) – into the A pentatonic minor scale, we get the 'blues scale'. Here it is starting on the sixth string:

 TRACK 17

And here is the A blues scale pattern that starts
on the 5th string:

TRACK 18

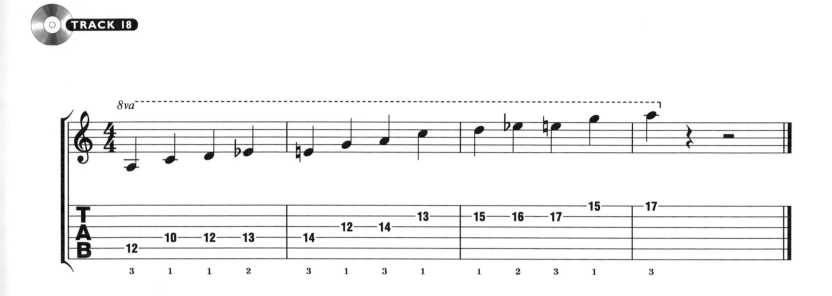

Here is the scale of A pentatonic major with the
root note on the 6th string:

TRACK 19

▶▶ **SANTANA**
"Blues to me comes from when a person can feel other people's pain and is able to articulate it. If you can feel the people's pain, like in Rwanda or on an Indian reservation, you can play some blues."

Here is the same scale starting with the root note A on the 5th string. This version of the scale sounds much higher.

TRACK 20

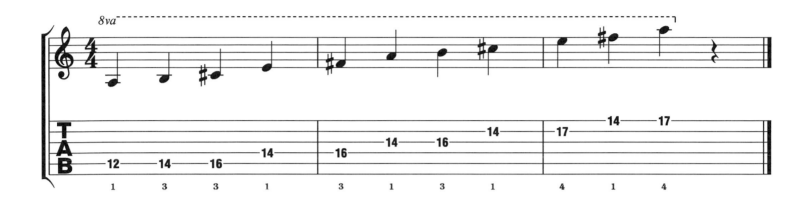

This is the scale of A natural minor with the root note on the 6th string. This has 7 notes, in contrast to the pentatonic's five. If you compare them – A B C D E F G with A C D E G – you'll see that the pentatonic minor is a sort of 'edited' version of the natural minor.

TRACK 21

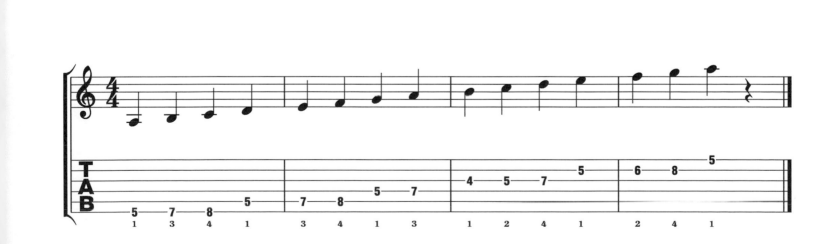

Here is the same scale starting with the root note
A on the 5th string:

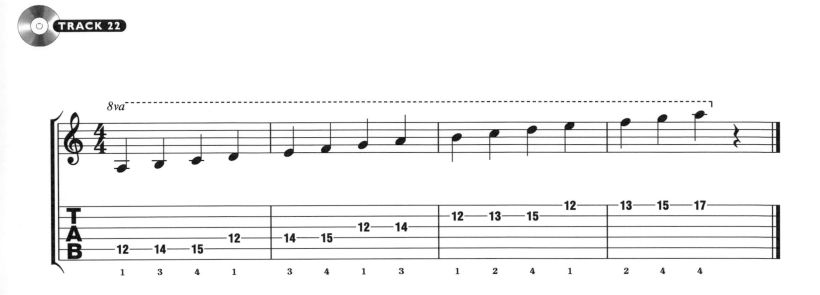

Now let's look at the scale of E pentatonic minor
with the root note on the open 6th string. This
'open' position is very common in blues guitar.

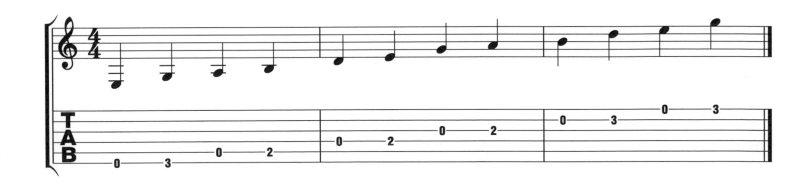

Here it is with the extension box to take you a bit
further up the neck:

TRACK 24

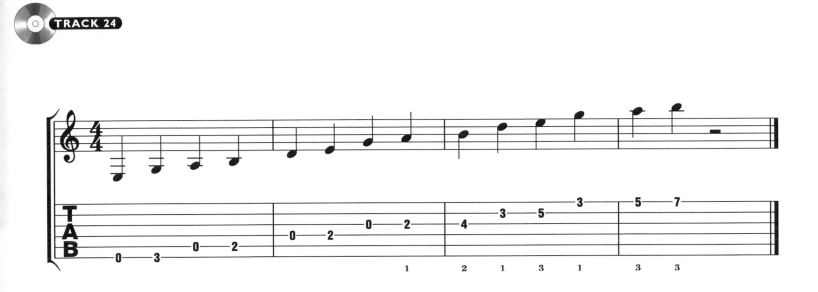

Next we insert a B♭ to turn this into the blues
scale for E:

TRACK 25

▶▶ **JIMI HENDRIX**
"You can have your own blues. Folk blues are not necessarily the only type of blues in the world... Everybody has some kind of blues to offer, you know."

It's important to distinguish between scales and scale patterns. The notes of an A major scale are the same for every musician regardless of what instrument they play, but a scale pattern on the guitar is obviously of no use to a violinist or a pianist. There are many ways of finding the notes for any given scale all over the fretboard – a scale pattern is just a convenient arrangement of the notes that is easy to remember.

With the exception of the last three E scales, the patterns above generally have no open strings in them. This means they are *movable*. If you need to play in a different key, you simply select the right scale for the key and move the pattern up or down until the starting note is the same as the key note. You have already been doing this in some of the exercises. As long as you play the pattern correctly all the notes will come out correctly for the new key.

You can now play patterns with the root note on either the 6th or 5th strings – so you have at least two places on the neck to play any given scale, one higher or lower than the other. Remember also that there are certain magic numbers which open up the fretboard – we've already seen how moving down three frets converts a pentatonic minor into the major form. Another magic number is 12:

If you move a scale pattern up or down the neck 12 frets (provided that you don't fall off either end), you will have moved the scale an octave higher or lower.

So the A pentatonic minor scale played at the 5th fret is made up of the same notes as one played 12 frets higher, at the 17th fret, but sounds an octave lower.

Played regularly with a metronome these patterns can help increase your speed. Increase the metronome speed gradually as you become more proficient.

▶▶ *JOHNNY WINTERS ON MUDDY WATERS*
"Out of all the blues singers, I don't think anyone can do more with one note than Muddy. And every note is blues whether voice or guitar."

The Blue House

You've probably heard a famous blues by Jimi Hendrix called *Red House*.

Welcome to the Blue House. Walk in, open each door and you'll find a different kind of blues. In this section you can try your hand at a variety of styles. You may well find that you'll hear traces of some famous players (and the way they approach the blues) in the following six pieces. Remember the patterns you've learnt and notice how parts of them are combined in practice. The challenge is to learn each individual phrase or bar and then put them together to form a longer stretch of music that lasts for more than 12 bars.

Muddy Country Blues

This type of blues was made famous by Muddy Waters and is based on a single one-bar riff using the chords E, A and G. The music stays hypnotically on this chord change underpinned by a strong beat. The key is E major and you'll see that this blues uses the E pentatonic minor and E blues scale in the open string position.

The two-note chords in the first bar are commonly used in the blues – these ones, played on the second and third strings, are immediately recognisable by their thick tone. Other notable features of *Muddy Country Blues* include the famous bluesy bend of the A in bar 2, and the microtone bend on G in bar 3. A microtone bend is a bend of less than a semitone, so the G isn't bent far enough to become G sharp. The smudging of the pitch which is created by a microtone bend is an authentic blues technique.

In bar 5 you'll notice that the top E occurs in two forms: fretted at the 5th fret, 2nd string, and as an open 1st string. Playing the same note as an open string and a fretted string creates a variety of tone. The open string has more brightness but the fretted equivalent can sound fuller and, of course, can be bent or treated with vibrato.

Bar 12 includes some more two-note chords – this time on the top two strings; compare the sound of these chords with those that started the track. Experiment with these ideas over the backing track. There is nothing to stop you venturing up the neck if you wish, say to E pentatonic minor at the 12th fret – just move the 5th fret A pentatonic minor up 7 frets.

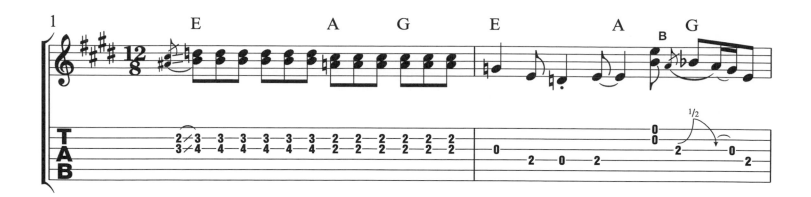

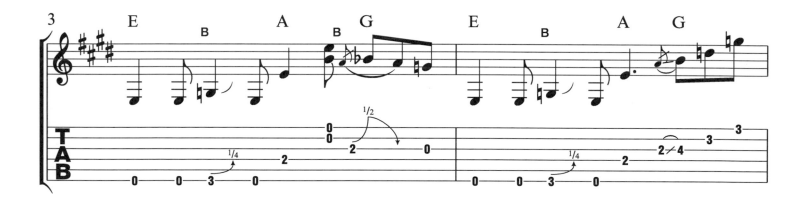

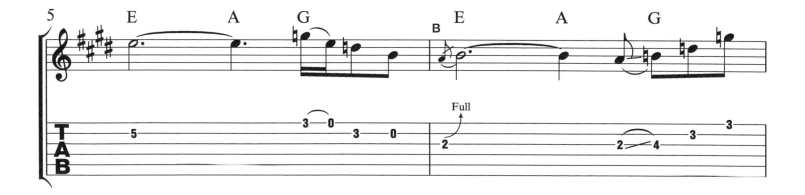

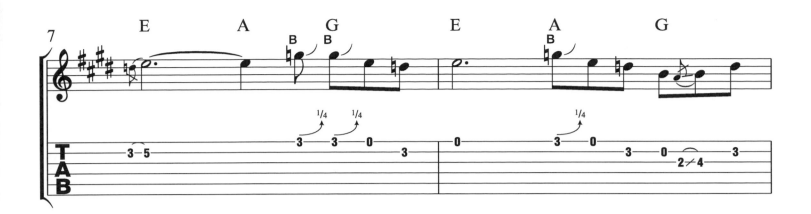

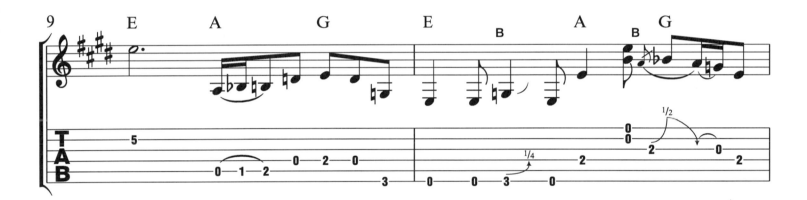

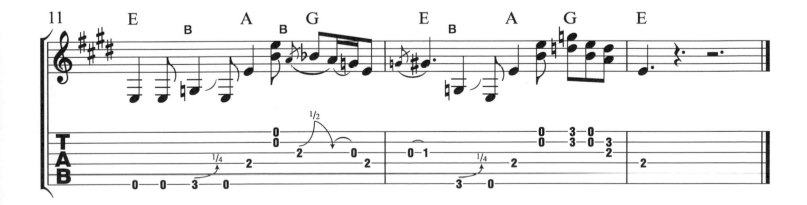

Flyover Blues

From the blues' rural origins we move into another room, where we find a supercharged heavy 60s blues. Much of *Flyover Blues* is played with the A pentatonic minor scale, although you will find some major phrases here and there to create moments of surprise – watch out for a C followed immediately by a C♯. You'll notice too that the phrases are longer in this piece than in the previous one.

The solos you have been playing so far have been scale-based – another approach is to split up chords and play their individual notes. This is called an arpeggio. Bars 1-2 use this technique – here, you're playing the three notes that make up an A7 chord.

Listen out for the psychedelic feel of the semitone bend in bar 3, the repeated bend in bars 13-14, and the shift onto the major pentatonic in bar 17. In bar 18 use your little finger to hold down the 17th fret on the 2nd string, while your 3rd finger bends the 3rd string at the 16th fret – your other two fingers should support the third finger on the same string.

Finally, in bars 21-22 you'll find a striking example of how bends give you more notes from the same fret! The C is bent a half-step, a whole step, then 1½ and finally 2 whole steps. It's a wild effect, but you'll need light gauge strings to be able to do it.

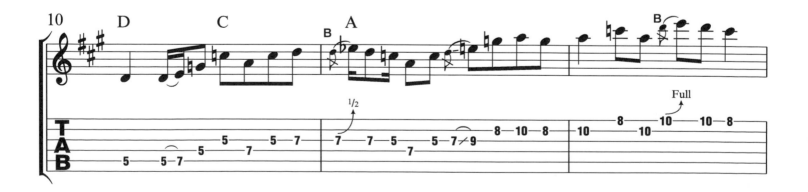

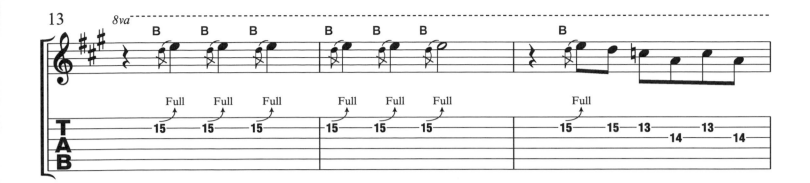

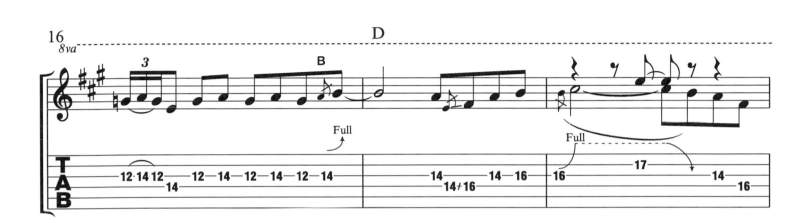

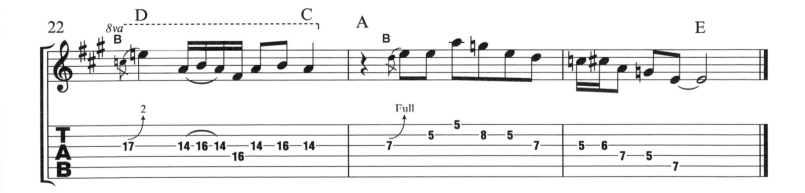

Turn The Lights Down Low

In a quiet room upstairs in the Blue House you'll find a romantic blues in the style of Peter Green, the 60s guitar legend of the original Fleetwood Mac. One of the hallmarks of his style is a sparing use of notes – not for him the long flowing lines of Clapton or Hendrix. Green places notes with the feeling of a man spending his last penny or dime, not knowing where the next one may come from. A characteristic of this kind of 'slow-burn' playing is the way sustained notes give way to the odd rapid sequence of notes, as in bar 7.

Unusually, this blues uses an 8-bar pattern, not a 12-bar. Notice, too, that the traditional 3-chord sequence has been expanded – it starts in A major, and then moves to D as you would expect, before returning to A via the 'flatter'

sound of F major. The mournful atmosphere is then emphasised by the inclusion of the chords of B minor and F# minor, as the sequence makes its way to the final E chord. The main scale used is A pentatonic major with occasional use of A pentatonic minor for a few bluesier flourishes here and there. Notice that the pentatonic major scale would not sound good over the minor chords in the sequence.

The most unusual moment in this piece comes in bars 13-14 where the scale passages give way to some simple intervals – an expressive shock to the ear. Notice also the bent note in the pair of notes in bar 16 – G natural rises a semitone to G# to give the correct note for an E chord.

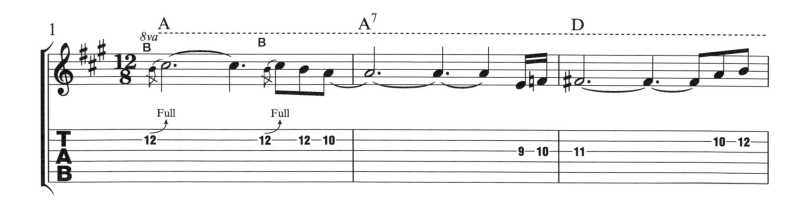

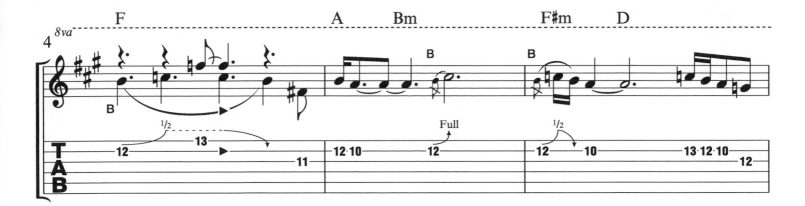

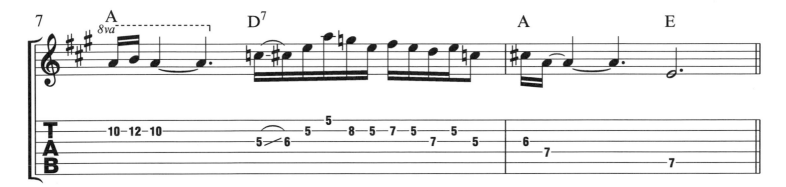

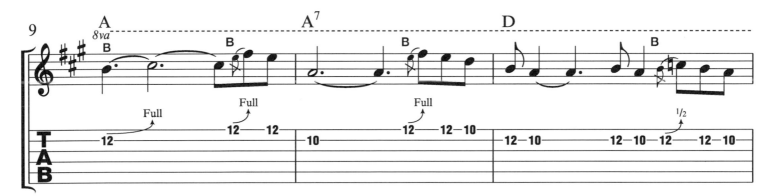

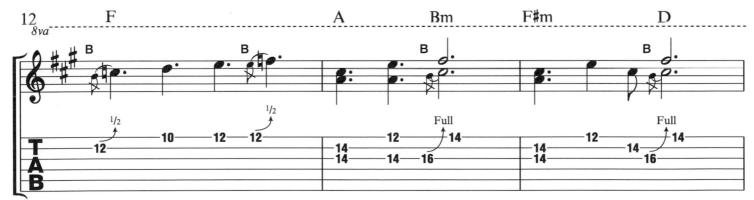

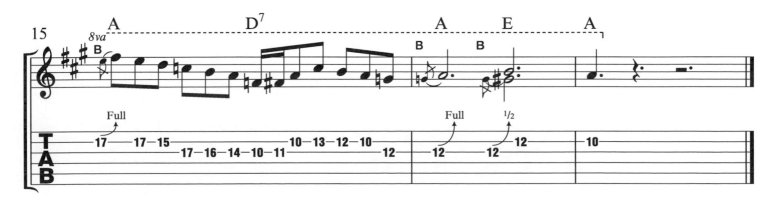

▶▶ STEVIE RAY VAUGHAN
"Most people can't bend my strings. The gauges I'm using now – .013, .016, .019, .028, .038, .056 – are small for me, but if I use them any bigger, I tear my fingers off."

Seattle To Texas

Downstairs, door right, you'll find this up-tempo
E blues. Jimi Hendrix and Stevie Ray Vaughan
were both masters of playing guitar parts that
suggested a lead guitarist and a rhythm guitarist
all in one – here's your chance to try your hand
at this style.

Seattle To Texas goes through the 12-bar
progression three times. Each phrase is followed
by a stab of chords. The trick is to be able to play
a lead phrase, grab the chords, then play another
lead phrase, then hit the chords, and so on,
without losing track of where you are.

For the first 24 bars the 'lead' phrases are played
low down, using the open position E pentatonic
minor and E blues scale patterns. In the last
12 bars the lead phrases move onto the higher
strings. In the last 12 bars, watch out for the
extra change to A (bar 27) – this is known as a
'quick-change' blues.

Notice how the last of each set of four chords
is tied across the bar-line, giving the music a
distinct 'push' each time it comes round.

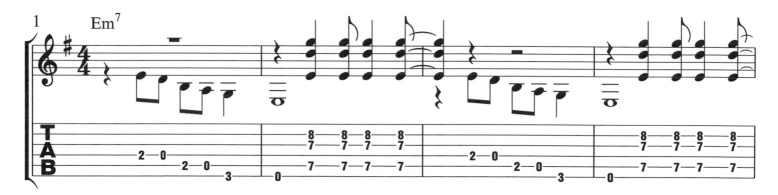

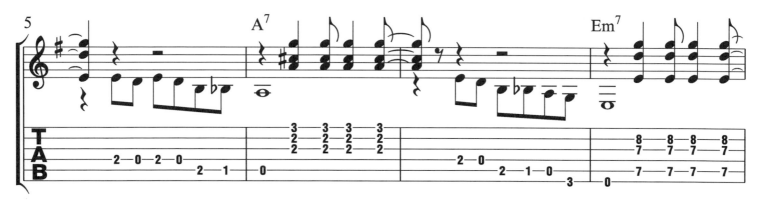

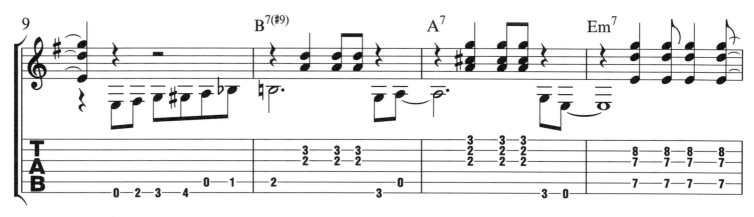

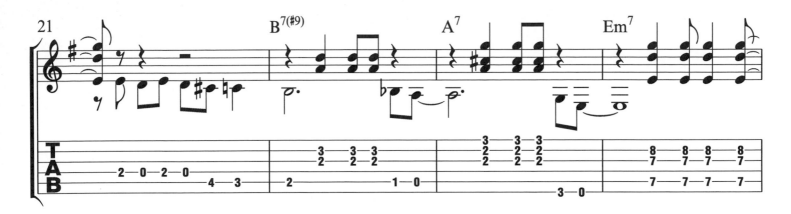

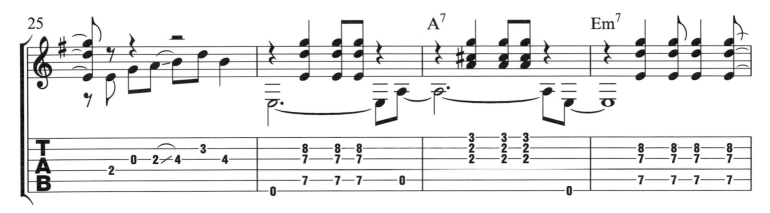

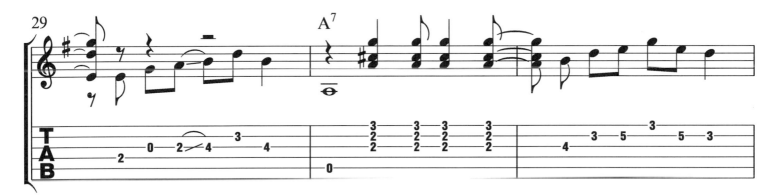

After The End

In the next dimly-lit room, we find *After The End*, another blues based on the expressive, atmospheric playing of Peter Green. In contrast to *Turn The Lights Down Low*, this is a minor key blues, using the chords of A minor, D minor and E minor. The emphasis here is on being as expressive as possible.

In this style of blues, the trick is to create tension by under-playing. Make the listener feel that you're about to explode any moment with a flurry of biting notes, but hold back. This piece uses A pentatonic minor and A natural minor too. The two extra notes – B and F – which the natural minor scale brings add a great deal to the feeling the music conveys. Listen for the tension of the unresolved B left hanging over A minor in bar 19.

As with *Flyover Blues* you'll find a couple of arpeggios. In bar 12, an A minor arpeggio leads into the second 12-bar progression, while in bar 16 you'll find another rising up a D minor chord at the 10th fret.

Rhythmically, watch out for the triplets in bars 9 and 18 , floating across the 4/4 beat.

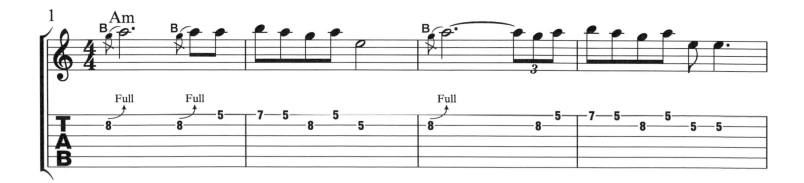

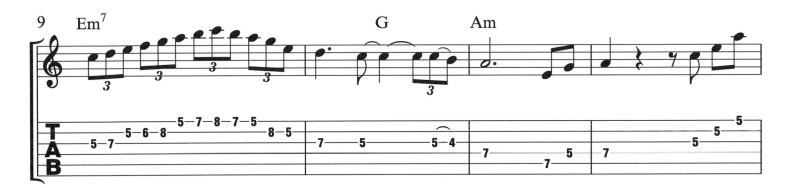

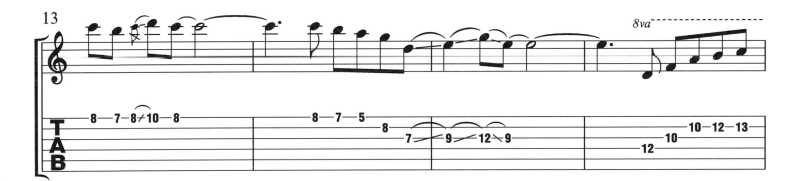

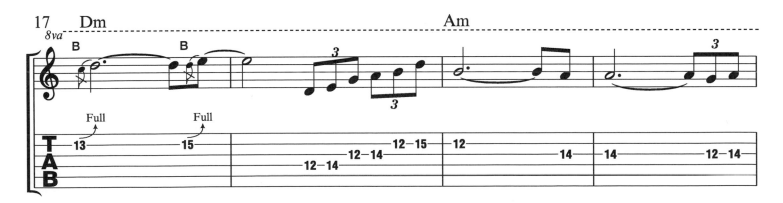

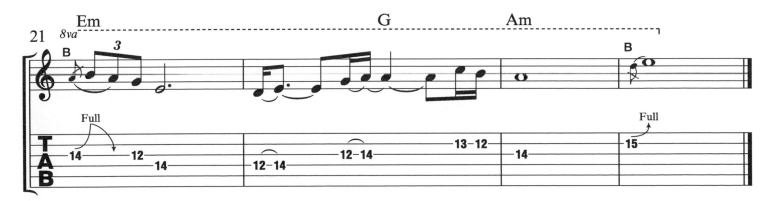

▶▶ **B.B. KING**

"Blues is a tonic for what ails you. It's for when you feel happy or sad.
People think that the blues is about a bunch of guys standing around and crying,
but that's just one side."

Soda Pop Blues

What's all that noise coming from the back room? Well, whaddaya know!? There's a party going on and it's time for you to join in. Contrary to its name, the blues isn't always sad – here's an up-tempo, swinging piece called *Soda Pop Blues* because it's light and bubbly.

Soda Pop Blues is in E major. There are 3 12-bar sequences and a bridge passage of 8 bars which briefly brings in a new key of B major.

This 12 bar progression will sound slightly different to what you're used to because the first 4 bars are played only with stabbed chords from the band: E in bar 1, A in bar 2, and E in bar 3. Bar 4 is left to the bass before the band enters properly at bar 5. These gaps in the backing create spaces for the soloist. Although you could play something in time with the chord stabs, it is more effective to wait and insert a phrase in the space between the chords – this creates a 'question and answer' dialogue between the soloist and band.

For the first 12 bars the main scale is E pentatonic major at the 9th fret. In bars 11-12 you'll find what is known as a 'turnaround' phrase – this finishes off the 12-bar sequence and brings you round to start the next one. There are two ways of playing notes together on the 1st and 3rd strings – either deaden the 2nd string inbetween by leaning the finger that's on the 3rd over a bit so it just makes contact, or, play the 3rd string note with your pick and use your 2nd or 3rd finger on the picking hand to pluck the 1st string simultaneously.

The second 12-bar sequence shifts to the E pentatonic minor scale while retaining some of the same musical ideas of the first 12 bars. The bridge begins at bar 25, and is designed to create some musical contrast to the 12-bar sequence. It begins with an A pentatonic major phrase at the 2nd fret, followed by a low-down E pentatonic major. Bars 31-32 show how an idea can be shifted around to match the chord changes.

The last 12 bar sequence starts off with some 2-note chords and a dramatic E9 chord. As *Soda Pop Blues* reaches its conclusion, you'll hear the effect of the contrast between major and minor scales.

▶▶ **ALBERT COLLINS**
"I tried using picks two or three times, man. I just don't like picks...
Picks will make you fast, though. But I really like digging in with my fingers."

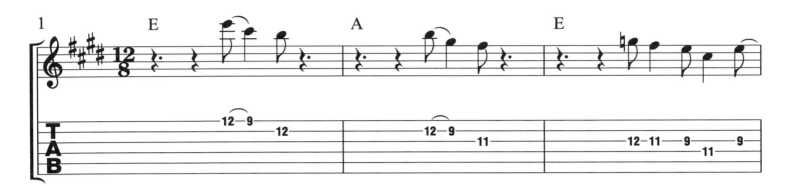

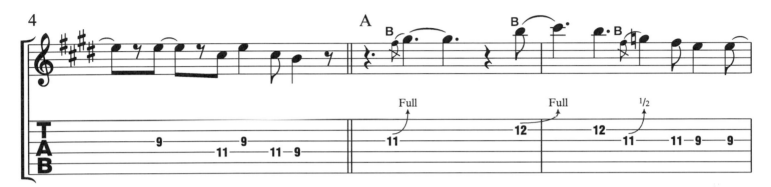

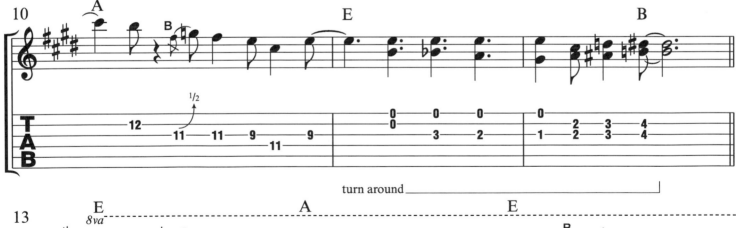

turn around

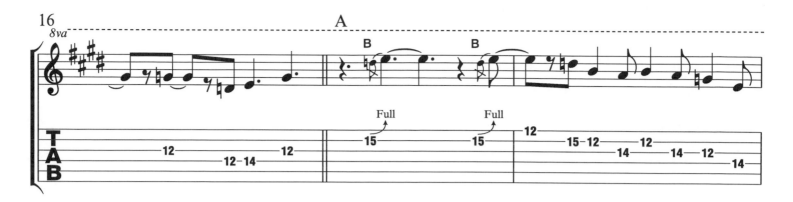

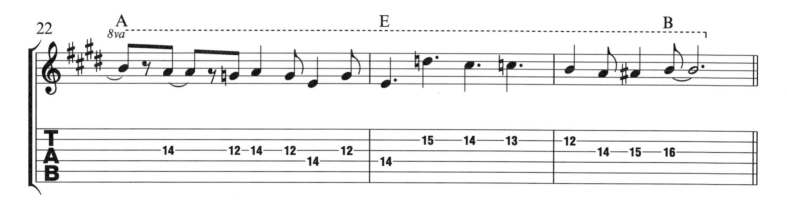

Bridge

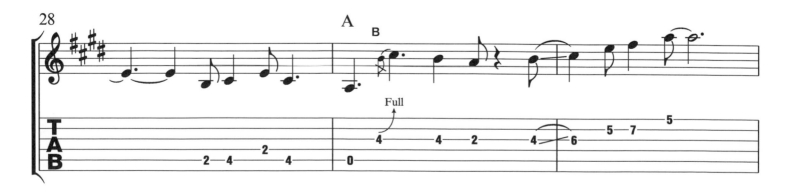

▶▶ SLASH

"I love R'n'B – the old rock and roll kind – like James Brown. I get a lot of rhythm ideas from that music. They're not note-for-note steals, but more the feel and mood – the groove."

Checklist

Let's recap on some of the points you've learned about blues soloing.

1. Select the right scale for the key:
   • For minor keys use the pentatonic minor, the blues scale, and the natural minor.

   • For blues in a major key use the pentatonic major, the blues scale, and the minor.

2. If you want to, you can stay on the same key scale for the whole 12-bar sequence. In more complicated blues, you need to watch out for any chords that are not in the key as these may necessitate some adjustments. You may also choose a scale to match the individual chords in a progression.

3. Remember that a pentatonic moved up or down 12 frets remains the same scale. It is shifted an octave higher or lower.

4. A pentatonic minor scale moved down 3 frets turns into the pentatonic major on the same note.

5. Don't forget arpeggios. Lead guitar doesn't just have to consist of scales. Try playing within a chord shape or using two notes at once.

6. Don't forget open strings – especially in the key of E major or E minor.

7. Bends are significant in blues for expression. Remember the microtone quarter-step bend, and the semitone, tone, and tone-and-a-half bends.

Choice Of Notes

Some important points to remember when you're trying to play a blues solo:

1. Melody. Can you whistle or sing parts of the solo?

2. Length. Should the solo be longer or shorter?

3. Phrasing. Try to make the phrasing as interesting as possible – use repetition, question and answer ideas, contrast scale movement with leaps, or play at different octaves.

4. Rhythm. Does the solo sit well with the rhythm of the backing?

5. Mood. Does the solo fit with the mood of the music?

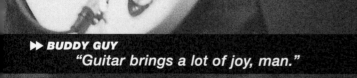

▶▶ **BUDDY GUY**
"Guitar brings a lot of joy, man."

Where Now?

If you've mastered the exercises and solos in this book you'll now have all the techniques and tricks you need to be able to play authentic blues guitar solos. If you want to know more, just listen to some of the musicians mentioned earlier, or check out some of the other music books available:

The Complete Guitar Player Blues Songbook
AM84484

The Complete Blues Guitar Player 1
AM91083

The Complete Blues Guitar Player 2
AM91084

The Complete Blues & Ragtime Guitar Player
AM62910

Learn To Play Power Blues Guitar Solos
AM91062 (Book + CD)

Blues Picture Chords And How To Use Them
AM21676

The Compact Blues Guitar Chord Reference
AM91731

The Anthology Of Blues Guitar
OK64973

Bottleneck Blues Guitar
OK64984

Contemporary Blues Guitar
AM934406

Country Blues Songbook
OK62588

Modern Blues For Guitar Tab 1
AM91515

Modern Blues For Guitar Tab 2
AM91763

Roots Of The Blues 1
SM11650

Roots Of The Blues 2
SM11668

Early Blues Songbook
AM29083

100 Rhythm & Blues Classics
AM85200

The Blues Bag
OK64991

Blues Guitar Inside & Out
CLM02509190

Blues Riffs For Guitar
AM23532

Blues You Can Use
HLE00695007 (Book + CD)

Robben Ford For Guitar Tab
AM92347

Go Solo! Blues Guitar
AM91418 (Book + CD)

Greatest Blues Solos For Guitar Tab
AM92398

B.B. King: King Of The Blues
AM92095

Ultimate Blues Guitar
HJ10124 (Book + CD)

Guitar Tablature Explained

Guitar music can be notated three different ways: on a musical stave, in tablature, and in rhythm slashes

RHYTHM SLASHES are written above the stave. Strum chords in the rhythm indicated. Round noteheads indicate single notes.

THE MUSICAL STAVE shows pitches and rhythms and is divided by lines into bars. Pitches are named after the first seven letters of the alphabet.

TABLATURE graphically represents the guitar fingerboard. Each horizontal line represents a string, and each number represents a fret.

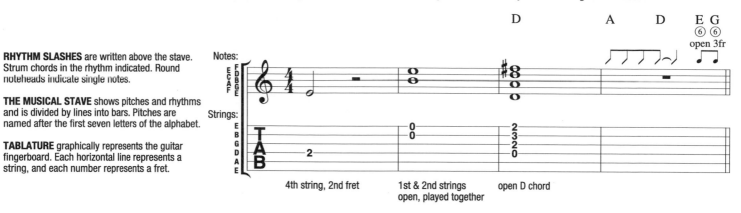

4th string, 2nd fret | 1st & 2nd strings open, played together | open D chord

definitions for special guitar notation

SEMI-TONE BEND: Strike the note and bend up a semi-tone (1/2 step).

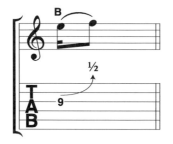

WHOLE-TONE BEND: Strike the note and bend up a whole-tone (whole step).

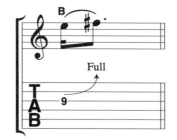

GRACE NOTE BEND: Strike the note and bend as indicated. Play the first note as quickly as possible.

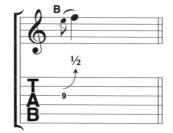

QUARTER-TONE BEND: Strike the note and bend up a 1/4 step.

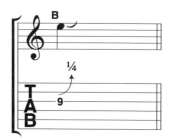

BEND & RELEASE: Strike the note and bend up as indicated, then release back to the original note.

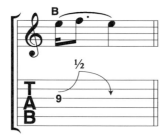

BEND & RESTRIKE: Strike the note and bend as indicated then restrike the string where the symbol occurs.

PRE-BEND: Bend the note as indicated, then strike it.

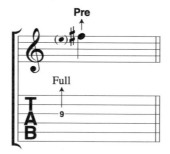

PRE-BEND & RELEASE: Bend the note as indicated. Strike it and release the note back to the original pitch.

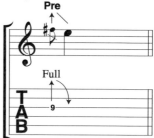

HAMMER-ON: Strike the first (lower) note with one finger, then sound the higher note (on the same string) with another finger by fretting it without picking.

PULL-OFF: Place both fingers on the notes to be sounded, Strike the first note and without picking, pull the finger off to sound the second (lower) note.

LEGATO SLIDE (GLISS): Strike the first note and then slide the same fret-hand finger up or down to the second note. The second note is not struck.

SHIFT SLIDE (GLISS & RESTRIKE): Same as legato slide, except the second note is struck.

NATURAL HARMONIC: Strike the note while the fret-hand lightly touches the string directly over the fret indicated.

PICK SCRAPE: The edge of the pick is rubbed down (or up) the string, producing a scratchy sound.

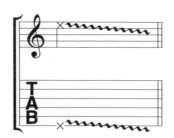

PALM MUTING: The note is partially muted by the pick hand lightly touching the string(s) just before the bridge.

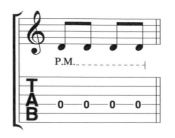

MUFFLED STRINGS: A percussive sound is produced by laying the fret hand across the string(s) without depressing, and striking them with the pick hand.

NOTE: The speed of any bend is indicated by the music notation and tempo.